Spotlight On

Civic Courage

Heroes of Conscience™

Raoul Wallenberg

Swedish Diplomat and Hero of the Holocaust

Lisa Idzikowski

Rosen YA™

New York

Published in 2018 by The Rosen Publishing Group, Inc.
29 East 21st Street, New York, NY 10010

First Edition

Library of Congress Cataloging-in-Publication Data

Names: Idzikowski, Lisa, author.
Title: Raoul Wallenberg : Swedish diplomat and hero of the Holocaust / Lisa Idzikowski.
Description: New York : Rosen Publishing Group, Inc., 2018. | Series: Spotlight on civic courage: heroes of conscience | Includes bibliographical references and index. | Audience: Grades 5–10.
Identifiers: LCCN 2017014239| ISBN 9781538381205 (library bound) | ISBN 9781538381175 (pbk.) | ISBN 9781538381182 (6 pack)
Subjects: LCSH: Wallenberg, Raoul, 1912–1947—Juvenile literature. | Righteous Gentiles in the Holocaust—Biography—Juvenile literature. | Diplomats—Sweden—Biography—Juvenile literature. | World War, 1939–1945—Jews—Rescue—Hungary—Juvenile literature. | Holocaust, Jewish (1939–1945)—Hungary—Juvenile literature. | Hungary—Ethnic relations—Juvenile literature.
Classification: LCC D804.66.W35 I39 2017 | DDC 940.53/18092 [B] —dc23
LC record available at https://lccn.loc.gov/2017014239

Manufactured in the United States of America

On the cover: Raoul Wallenberg, shown in this photo from around 1937, worked tirelessly to save about one hundred thousand Hungarian Jews from being sent to death camps. The background photo depicts Jews from Hungary destined for an extermination camp.

CONTENTS

HEROIC SAVIOR

Imagine sitting in the largest stadium in the United States. Slightly more than one hundred thousand people fit in Michigan Stadium, at the University of Michigan. Now imagine those thousands of people are rounded up and exterminated.

Toward the end of World War II, Adolf Hitler and his Nazi regime had already murdered most of Europe's Jewish population. All that remained was the very large population of Jews living in Hungary. The War Refugee Board (WRB) searched for someone to prevent this mass extermination.

Coming from an upper-class, well-known banking family in Sweden, Raoul Wallenberg volunteered to jump into the lion's den that was Budapest, Hungary. Tirelessly, he waged war against the Nazi killing machine. Wallenberg's struggle lasted nearly six months, before the Soviet forces captured Budapest. In the end, Raoul Wallenberg managed to save about 100,000 of Hungary's 825,000 Jews.

Tragically, Raoul Wallenberg vanished and was never heard from again.

As a young man, Raoul Wallenberg became interested in working against cruelty and injustice. During World War II, he struggled to save Jewish citizens in Budapest, Hungary.

Raoul's Beginning

Raoul Wallenberg's birth on August 4, 1912, in Stockholm, Sweden, was an occasion of tremendous joy, as his mother welcomed her firstborn son. It was also a time of immense sorrow because she mourned her recently deceased husband.

As a little boy, the fatherless Raoul lived with his mother and grandmother. At his grandmother's beachfront property, the young boy played, climbed, hiked, and picked berries. Raoul enjoyed time with his cousin, and they often walked together to a nearby park and their gymnastics lessons.

Raoul's paternal grandfather was a diplomat. He lived in other countries but visited his grandson whenever he came home to Sweden. Grandfather Gustav cared for Raoul and was happy to see his grandson becoming an independent youngster who was learning English.

On October 5, 2015, Australia issued a postage stamp recognizing Raoul Wallenberg's achievements. Previously, Australia had honored Wallenberg by naming him an honorary citizen.

Young Raoul knew his father only from a portrait that hung above the bed. By the age of six, Raoul had two fathers—the one in his heart and his mother's new husband.

Favorite Subjects

In his elementary school years, Raoul often collected stamps and spent time with his half-brother and half-sister. He also enjoyed wandering around Stockholm. Along the way, Raoul investigated various building projects and questioned construction workers. Unlike many Swedish boys his age, Raoul hardly ever played soccer. In school, he was not particularly good at math, but he gradually found that he enjoyed—and was good at—singing and drawing.

Raoul also showed a knack for learning foreign languages, which his mother and grandfather proudly encouraged. One summer, Raoul spent several weeks in Germany improving his understanding of the German language. During another vacation, he lived with a family in France. While there, besides practicing French, Raoul befriended a fellow student, a Jewish boy from Hungary.

As a teenager, Raoul made an exciting discovery about himself: Architecture, travel, languages, drawing, and meeting new people were what made him happy.

Raoul Wallenberg adored his half-siblings. For many years, Wallenberg's half-sister Nina Lagergren searched for any bit of information in the hope of finding her brother.

Traveling Afar

Raoul followed his grandfather's advice about education and work experience. At his urging, Raoul marched off to military training, attended college in America, and spent time in faraway cities learning about banking and business.

Seventeen-year-old Raoul served in Sweden's Royal Life Guard Regiment, and after completing this compulsory training, he launched into architecture at the University of Michigan. The drawings and paintings of the hardworking Rudy, as he was called, impressed his professors. He graduated at the top of his class and later accepted a medal from the American Institute of Architects.

Grandfather Gustav's arranged business and banking internships were next on Raoul Wallenberg's agenda. First, he sailed to Cape Town, South Africa, and worked in sales. But he found this work not challenging enough. So he pushed ahead to an internship in banking in Haifa, in British-controlled Palestine.

Raoul gained significant insights from these experiences. He discovered empathy for the Jewish people and their suffering, and he also realized that banking was not the career for him.

Military training was compulsory in Sweden, and Raoul Wallenberg served his first assignment after high school.

What to Do Now?

But Wallenberg suddenly lost his way. His stern, loving, guiding force of a grandfather became ill and died. What would he do now?

No longer receiving an allowance from his grandfather, Wallenberg had to find a job. He knocked on the door of every possible employer in Sweden's capital. He didn't have any luck. Swedish firms refused to hire an architect trained in the United States. They didn't think an American architectural degree was good enough.

Around this same time, Adolf Hitler enacted the Nuremberg Race Laws in Germany. Many people in Europe felt lost, confused, and afraid. Just three years later, Nazi forces occupied Austria. These newly initiated laws enforced crippling restrictions and encouraged hatred and violence against Jewish citizens.

In an effort to prevent war, diplomats from Britain, France, and Germany signed the Munich Agreement. For Hitler, this meant that he had agreed to expand into the Sudetenland section of Czechoslovakia but no farther.

Raoul Wallenberg enjoyed his college years at the University of Michigan, but he missed his home in Sweden. Wallenberg loved outdoor sports, such as biking and sailing.

In the Army

Hitler did not honor the Munich Agreement. Greedy to expand his territory, he seized the rest of Czechoslovakia in 1939. Six months later, when Germany's Wehrmacht invaded Poland, Britain and France declared war on Germany. World War II had begun.

Swedes rushed to stockpile groceries, and soon shelves were emptied of tea, coffee, sugar, spices, and soap. The Swedish government drafted men into the military. And Raoul Wallenberg prepared himself for the possibility of going to war.

Wallenberg's first experience in the military had been after high school. He had worked with machine guns and demonstrated a talent for marksmanship, or shooting. He had even earned a silver medal for it. Now at the beginning of the war, his unit, the Svea Life Guards (SLGs), was called up for duty. The SLG protected Stockholm, the Swedish capital, and trained volunteers in the Home Guard. Sergeant Wallenberg specialized in drills, preparing men for battle in urban settings.

Adolf Hitler and other Nazi officials are shown here witnessing the signing of the Munich Agreement by French premier Edouard Daladier.

Is This Sweden?

Hitler and his Nazi war machine appeared unstoppable. Some seven months after World War II had begun, German boots pounded through Denmark and Norway. Conflict edged closer, and all of Sweden wondered what would happen next. Would they be invaded?

Discussions were happening all over Sweden—among the people and in the government. At all costs, the prime minister wished to keep Sweden safe, avoid fighting, and avoid angering Germany. The government reaffirmed Sweden's neutrality.

For many years, the population of Sweden had hardly changed. Few people moved into or out of this harsh, northern land, so Sweden's culture contained little or no diversity, or variety. Many Swedes mistrusted foreigners and immigrants. They argued against accepting war refugees, especially Jews fleeing German-occupied territories.

Wallenberg challenged these ideas, welcomed diversity, and rejected anti-Semitism. Besides his positive experiences with people from other countries and fluency in French, German, English, and Russian, Wallenberg himself had Jewish ancestry.

Raoul Wallenberg's mother proudly encouraged his achievements and celebrated with him after graduation in 1930.

In 1941, the war escalated, or became more intense. Hitler broke his treaty with the Soviet Union and launched a surprise attack. As Germany's ally, Hungary sent troops to fight the Soviets and tightened its laws against the Jews at home.

In Sweden, everything was rationed. The availability of tea, coffee, bread, butter, meat, eggs, and cheese in people's kitchens depended on ration coupons, not what they wished to purchase.

Two entrepreneurs in Sweden searched for ways to increase food supplies. They formed a partnership to import and export goods between Sweden and several European countries. In order to succeed, they needed to hire someone with travel, business, and foreign language experience. Luckily, they were put in touch with the perfect candidate!

By August 1941, Wallenberg had secured his first full-time job in international sales and trade as foreign director of the Mid-European Trading Company (METC). Not long afterward, Germany declared war on the United States.

Raoul Wallenberg was ready for a full-time job. He landed a position as an international salesman using his superior language skills and natural ability to work well with people.

Can It Be True?

Businessman Raoul Wallenberg settled into his job at the Mid-European Trading Company. By day, he exported and imported an assortment of goods. After work, he trained members of Sweden's Home Guard. Neutrality did not guarantee safety, and Sweden improved its defenses in case of war.

To conduct business, Wallenberg traveled to Germany, France, and Hungary. As a main supplier for the METC, Hungary exported an impressive variety of food. Wallenberg imported chickens, turkeys, geese, egg products, and preserved vegetables for thankful Swedes. As a salesman, he dealt with businessmen, diplomats, and politicians in the Hungarian capital of Budapest. As the kind and friendly person he was, Wallenberg frequently visited his associates' Jewish relatives living there.

Wallenberg, like many people, tried to stay informed about the war. Unfortunately, not all events appeared in

As an international salesman, Raoul Wallenberg refined his skills in organization and negotiation, which he later put to good use as a diplomat, seen here, serving in Budapest, Hungary.

the news or on the radio. Previously, Hitler had issued an order to top Nazi officials: exterminate all European Jews. A month later, in January 1942, these officials convened the Wannsee Conference, where they organized details of Hitler's Final Solution.

There are many monuments around the world that pay tribute to the heroic efforts of Raoul Wallenberg, including this sculpture in New York City.

Reports of Germany's genocidal actions began reaching the outside world. They outraged government officials, and citizens demanded action. Sweden informed the Germans that it would now harbor any Jewish refugees fleeing persecution.

During his recent travels to Hungary, Wallenberg had witnessed the deteriorating conditions in Budapest. He vowed to help in some way. One night, Raoul Wallenberg was invited to watch a secret screening of the movie *Pimpernel Smith*. In it, the heroic main character outsmarts the Germans and rescues Jews from the Nazis. That was it! Wallenberg knew he would someday be that hero.

Meanwhile, the war raged on. Finally, the Allied forces delivered several smashing defeats to the seemingly unstoppable Germans. Hitler's allies took notice, and Hungary secretly sent representatives to forge peace with the United States and Britain.

Finding His Calling

As Germany suffered wider defeat, Hitler demanded stricter enforcement of anti-Semitic laws and more soldiers to fight the Soviets. Hungary had already enacted harsh anti-Semitic laws affecting its Jewish citizens. When Hitler insisted that Admiral Miklós Horthy enact the Final Solution for Hungary's Jews, the brave regent refused. (When a king, queen, or other ruler is unable to lead for some reason, a regent is the person who governs in his or her place.)

Finally, Hitler was fed up. After learning of Horthy's secret peace negotiations with the Allies, German troops invaded Hungary. A pro-German ruler was appointed, and the Nazis accelerated their objective of *judenrein*. Hungary's 825,000 Jews would be deported to the Auschwitz concentration camp and killed.

The world objected. US president Franklin Roosevelt directed his War Refugee Board (WRB) to intervene. The

WRB officials contacted Wallenberg, hammered out a plan, and organized a mission. Wallenberg agreed, but he had one condition: he must be allowed to use any methods, including bribery and threats, to save as many Hungarian Jews as possible. Wallenberg packed the essentials, including a nine-millimeter revolver!

Miklós Horthy served as an admiral in the Hungarian Navy before being elected by the Hungarian Parliament to the office of regent, or ruler, of Hungary.

On the Way to Budapest

The Germans lost no time after invading Hungary. Under the command of Schutzstaffel (SS) officer Adolf Eichmann, roundups and deportations to temporary camps were followed by train transport to Auschwitz. This happened almost overnight. Restrictions allowed Jews to move around the city for only about three hours a day. And with few exceptions, Jewish citizens had to affix an identifying patch to their clothing—the yellow star.

Thousands upon thousands of individuals and families were deported from the Hungarian countryside to their deaths. President Franklin Roosevelt intervened again. He used the radio and printed leaflets smuggled through the underground or dropped from planes to demand that the deportations halt. Roosevelt threatened the perpetrators of the Holocaust with eventual punishment as mass murderers. Sweden's king Gustav V also dispatched a letter to Regent Horthy, begging him to find some way to halt

In preparation for his humanitarian mission to Hungary, Raoul Wallenberg was issued a diplomatic passport before leaving for the Swedish legation in Hungary.

the atrocities. German-friendly politicians were in charge, but Horthy had so much support among the Hungarian Army and others that he managed to get a temporary stop to the transports.

Name: Judith Kopstein
Név:
Wohnort: Budgest
Lakás:
Geburtsdatum: 30. Jan 1930
Születési ideje:
Geburtsort: Budapest
Születési helye:
Körperlänge: 171 cm
Magasság:
Haarfarbe: blond Augenfarbe: blau
Hajszín: Szemszín:

Unterschrift: Judith Kopstein
Aláírás:

SCHWEDEN SVÉDORSZÁG

Die Kgl. Schwedische Gesandtschaft in Budapest bestätigt, dass der Obengenannte im Rahmen der — von dem Kgl. Schwedischen Aussenministerium autorisierten — Repatriierung nach Schweden reisen wird. Der Betreffende ist auch in einen Kollektivpass eingetragen.

Bis Abreise steht der Obengenannte und seine Wohnung unter dem Schutz der Kgl. Schwedischen Gesandtschaft in Budapest.

Gü...
nach Sch...

A budapesti Svéd Kir. Követség igazolja, hogy fentnevezett — a Svéd Kir. Külügyminisztérium által jóváhagyott — repatriálás keretében Svédországba utazik.

Nevezett a kollektív útlevélben is szerepel.

Elutazásdig fentnevezett és lakása a budapesti Svéd Kir. Követség oltalma alatt áll.

...eszti a Svédországba való megérke... ...tizennegyedik napon.

Reisebere... ...in dem Kollektivpass eingetragen.

Budapest, den 20. August 194...

KÖNIGLICH SCHWEDISCHE GESANDTSCHAFT
SVÉD KIRÁLYI KÖVETSÉG

Shortly after arriving in Budapest, Raoul Wallenberg designed a new protective passport, the Schutz-Pass, in hopes of protecting Jewish citizens from deportation.

By the time Wallenberg arrived for his mission to Budapest on Sunday, July 9, 1944, about four hundred thousand Jewish lives had been lost. This propelled him into immediate action. Wallenberg organized a new department at the Swedish legation, Section C—the humanitarian department. He designed a new and improved protective pass, the Schutz-Pass, intended to guarantee protection under the Swedish legation for individuals and their residences. He also met with and sized up various officials, determining whom he could successfully bribe or threaten.

The WRB originally expected that Wallenberg would move Jews out of Hungary to safety. But he quickly saw a better way. A greater number could be saved if he found a way to protect them right there in Budapest. But Wallenberg had to hurry; the deportations could begin again at any time!

Wallenberg's Surprise

Raoul Wallenberg was surprised by the string of events stretching from summer to mid-autumn 1944. Romania dropped the first bombshell by declaring war on Germany. And two German allies, Bulgaria and Finland, jumped ship. When the western Allies arrived in Paris, they liberated the city.

Hungary's regent wasted no time in taking advantage of the Germans' weakness. Admiral Horthy evicted the pro-German government and installed a handpicked minister. Guided by Horthy, the new government halted deportations. The Hungarians attempted to convince the Germans of their loyalty as an ally, but it was a ruse, or a trick. Horthy again approached the Allies seeking peace and sent a secret envoy to treaty with the Soviets.

Surprisingly, Germany's SS leader did not reinstate the deportations. He was busy negotiating peace with the

West behind Hitler's back. He probably thought he might get better results if the killing stopped.

Approximately two hundred thousand Jews remained in Budapest, and Wallenberg worked tirelessly to save their lives.

Raoul Wallenberg was serious about saving the Jewish citizens of Budapest. He acted quickly and decisively to rescue as many as possible.

Not Over Yet

At lunchtime on October 15, 1944, Admiral Horthy announced that Hungary had signed an armistice with the Soviet Union. People rejoiced—the war was over! Not surprisingly, the Germans had long known of Horthy's deal and had prepared for the regent's defection, or desertion.

Shortly before the admiral's announcement, German SS soldiers whisked his captured son off to a concentration camp in Austria. The next morning, Horthy surrendered and was arrested. In exchange for his son's life, the admiral proclaimed an Arrow Cross member the new leader of Hungary.

The Hungarian Arrow Cross, or Nyilas, was a terrifying group. They were highly anti-Semitic. As they roamed the streets, they tortured and killed Jews with no regard for the protective passes distributed by Raoul Wallenberg and the other legations.

In better times, before the outbreak of World War II, Admiral Horthy kept in contact with many European leaders.

With the Nyilas in power, Adolf Eichmann returned to Budapest and resumed the deportations. Now, deportees were forced to walk to the Austrian border before boarding death trains.

More Danger, More Challenges

The dangers and challenges for Raoul Wallenberg and his humanitarian department intensified. He raced from one task to the next. Through negotiation, threats, and bribery, Wallenberg attempted to save all the people he could from the bloodthirsty Nyilas, forced labor details, deportation, sickness, and starvation.

Section C now employed more than three hundred Jewish volunteers. Thirty-one "Swedish Houses" containing eight thousand to nine thousand Jews with passports issued from the Swedish legation made up the international ghetto. Between seventy thousand and one hundred thousand Jews without protective passports from one of the legations crowded into another area, known as the general ghetto.

One day, Raoul Wallenberg made an unusual request. He wanted a photographer colleague to document the events happening all around Budapest. Wallenberg knew that postwar retribution would depend upon solid proof.

The photographer snapped away as the roar of artillery erupted day and night. By November, the Soviet army battled only nine miles (fourteen kilometers) from the capital city.

From his desk at the Swedish legation, Raoul Wallenberg administered his humanitarian department, Section C, with competent skill.

Efforts Amid Chaos

Dead people, dead animals, and house rubble covered Budapest's streets as constant gunshots whistled through the air. Wallenberg soldiered on, disregarding death threats and living through several attempts to kill him that were disguised as accidents. By Christmas week, high-ranking Hungarian, German, and Arrow Cross leaders and diplomats had rushed to flee the Soviet-surrounded city. Red Army units would soon block the last road out.

On Christmas Eve, Arrow Cross thugs mounted an attack against Wallenberg and the Swedish legation. Two members were captured and marched off, while others managed to evade the Nyilas. After getting back together, the Swedish staff discussed how they would hold out until the Soviets took control.

As a last evil act, German and Arrow Cross soldiers prepared to murder all the Jews in the main ghetto. A legation confidant convinced the German general in charge that Wallenberg would see him convicted of war crimes. The attack was called off!

An award-winning television movie portrays Raoul Wallenberg and dramatizes his heroic efforts to save Hungarian Jews from destruction.

What Happened to Raoul Wallenberg?

Wallenberg's last letter to his mother left for Sweden on December 8, 1944, in the final diplomatic bag out of Budapest. He described his situation as exciting and dangerous, wished her a good New Year, enclosed two recent photos, and said that he would not be home for some time.

Planning ahead for the Soviet takeover, Wallenberg designed a postwar assistance program financed by money from Roosevelt's War Refugee Board. The Wallenberg Institution for Aid and Reconstruction would provide assistance to Hungary's Jewish population to rebuild their lives.

Continuous combat ravaged the Budapest neighborhood where Raoul Wallenberg hid and waited. On January 13, 1945, soldiers broke into the building. The secretary presented his diplomatic identification and asked to speak with a superior. At first, it appeared that Wallenberg would meet the Soviet commander. But four days later, an arrest order was issued. Wallenberg boarded a train bound for Moscow and disappeared.

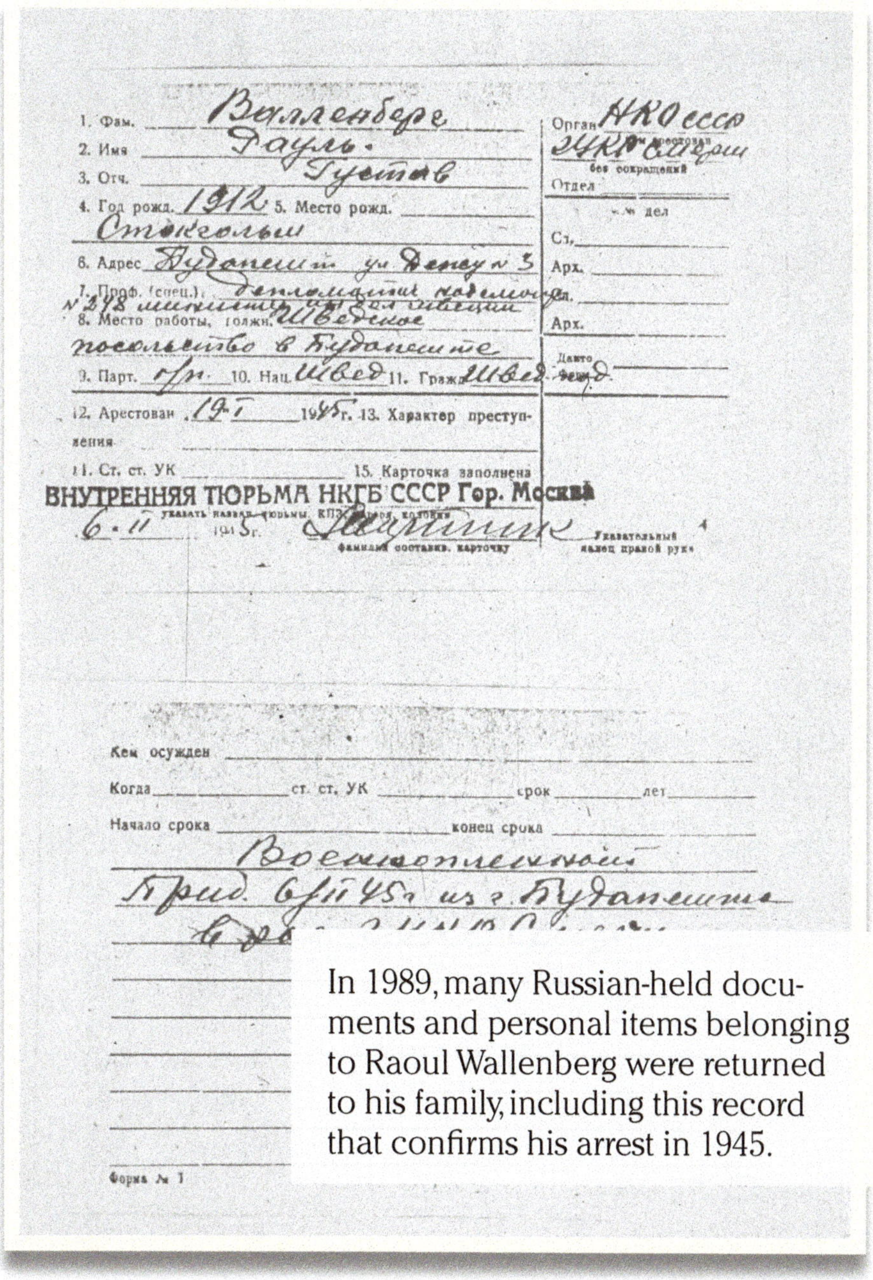
1. Фам.
2. Имя
3. Отч.
4. Год рожд. 5. Место рожд.
6. Адрес
7. Проф. (спец.)
8. Место работы, должн.
9. Парт. 10. Нац. 11. Гражд.
12. Арестован 13. Характер преступления
14. Ст. ст. УК 15. Карточка заполнена
ВНУТРЕННЯЯ ТЮРЬМА НКГБ СССР Гор. Москва
фамилия составит. карточку
Указательный палец правой руки
Орган
без сокращений
Отдел
Ст.
Арх.
Арх.
Кем осужден
Когда ст. ст. УК срок лет
Начало срока конец срока
Форма № 1

In 1989, many Russian-held documents and personal items belonging to Raoul Wallenberg were returned to his family, including this record that confirms his arrest in 1945.

Gone but Never Forgotten

At first, Wallenberg's family received news that he was alive and under Soviet protection. Everyone waited for him to return to Sweden. His family, friends, and closest legation colleague, Per Anger, pressured the Soviets with letters and calls. But Wallenberg never returned home.

Since the end of the war, numerous conflicting reports and information have surrounded Wallenberg's disappearance. For years, the Soviets claimed he had died in prison in Moscow. Uncovered facts show that they lied: after his arrest, Wallenberg was transferred from one prison to another. According to evidence from other prisoners and their sightings of Wallenberg, he survived for many years in confinement. We may never know for certain when Wallenberg passed away.

Wallenberg's heroic spirit lives on in all the descendants of the Hungarian Jews he saved. Forever a hero, he is honored as "righteous among the nations" of Israel and as an honorary citizen of the United States.

A large stained-glass mural in the Raoul Wallenberg Holocaust Memorial Park near the Great Synagogue in Budapest, Hungary, reminds the world of Wallenberg's heroic deeds.

GLOSSARY

anti-Semitism Opposition or hostility toward Jewish people.

armistice When opponents agree to stop acts of warfare.

Arrow Cross (Nyilas) Anti-Semitic Hungarians who identified with the Nazis of Germany.

atrocities Very cruel, terrible acts.

Auschwitz The German concentration camp in Poland where many people were murdered.

compulsory Required to do or complete.

diplomat A person who works to represent his or her government in other countries.

exterminate To get rid of completely, usually by killing.

Final Solution Hitler's plan to exterminate all Jewish people living in Europe.

genocidal Describes the action of deliberately killing one particular group of people.

ghetto The part of a city, often dirty and crowded, where a minority group, such as Jews, were required to live.

Holocaust The mass killing of Jews and other groups of people by the Nazis in World War II.

Home Guard The men who volunteered to protect Sweden during World War II.

Judenrein A German word that means to be free of Jews.

legation A group of diplomats working in a foreign country.

neutrality When a country maintains a stance to not take sides to avoid war.

Nuremberg Laws Rules instigated by the Nazis against the Jews in 1935.

Schutzstaffel (SS) A special group in the Nazi military that controlled and persecuted Jewish people.

War Refugee Board (WRB) Group appointed by President Franklin Roosevelt to assist war refugees.

Wehrmacht The armed forces of Nazi Germany.

yellow star Yellow star-shaped identification patch worn by Jews in German-occupied countries during World War II.

FOR MORE INFORMATION

Friends of Simon Wiesenthal Center for Holocaust Studies: Canada
5075 Yonge Street, Suite 902
Toronto, ON M2N 6C6
Canada
(866) 864-9735
Email: swcmain@fswc.ca
Website: https://www.friendsofsimonwiesenthalcenter.com
Facebook: @CanadianFriendsofSimonWiesenthalCenter
Twitter: @CanadianFSWC
The Friends of Simon Wiesenthal Center is dedicated to stamping out anti-Semitism and advancing freedom, democracy, and human rights for all people.

International Raoul Wallenberg Foundation
34 East 67th Street
New York, NY 10065
(212) 737-3275
Website: http://www.raoulwallenberg.net
Facebook: @TheInternationalRaoulWallenbergFoundation
Twitter: @TheIRWF
The International Raoul Wallenberg Foundation aims to educate and increase public awareness based on the values shared by heroes of the Holocaust.

Raoul Wallenberg Committee of the United States
37 West 26th Street, Suite 403
New York, NY 10010
(646) 678-3711
Website: http://www.raoulwallenberg.org
The Raoul Wallenberg Committee of the United States works to promote the nonviolent courage of Raoul Wallenberg and to demonstrate to the world that a single person has the power to make a difference.

Yad Vashem—World Holocaust Remembrance Center
The Holocaust Martyrs' and Heroes' Remembrance Authority
Har Hazikaron
P.O.B. 3477
Jerusalem 9103401
Israel
Website: http://www.yadvashem.org
Facebook: @yadvashem
Twitter: @yadvashem
Instagram: @yadvashem
The World Holocaust Remembrance Center encourages awareness and remembrance of all those involved in the Holocaust.

Websites

Because of the changing nature of Internet links, Rosen Publishing has developed an online list of websites related to the subject of this book. This site is updated regularly. Please use this link to access this list:

http://www.rosenlinks.com/CIVC/Wallenberg

FOR FURTHER READING

Borden, Louise. *His Name Was Raoul Wallenberg: Courage, Rescue and Mystery During World War II.* Boston, MA: Houghton Mifflin, 2012.

Brezina, Corona. *Nazi Architects of the Holocaust* (A Documentary History of the Holocaust). New York, NY: Rosen Publishing, 2015.

Deem, James. *Auschwitz: Voices from the Death Camp.* Berkeley Heights, NJ: Enslow Publishing, 2015.

Glick, Susan. *Heroes of the Holocaust.* San Diego, CA: Lucent Books, 2003.

Greek, Joe. *Righteous Gentiles.* New York, NY: Rosen Publishing, 2015.

Linnea, Sharon. *Raoul Wallenberg: The Man Who Stopped Death.* Philadelphia, PA: The Jewish Publication Society, 1993.

Lowery, Zoe. *The Nazi Regime and the Holocaust.* (Bearing Witness: Genocide and Ethnic Cleansing in the Modern World). New York, NY: Rosen Publishing, 2017.

Simon, Emma, and Thomas Streissguth. *Raoul Wallenberg* (The Holocaust). New York, NY: The Rosen Publishing Group, 2016.

BIBLIOGRAPHY

Anger, Per. *With Raoul Wallenberg in Budapest*. New York, NY: Holocaust Library, 1981.

Bierman, John. *Righteous Gentile*. New York, NY: The Viking Press, 1981.

Carlberg, Ingrid. *Raoul Wallenberg: The Biography*. New York, NY: MacLehose Press, 2015.

Carlberg, Ingrid. "Raoul Wallenberg's Biographer Uncovers Important Clues to What Happened in His Final Days." Smithsonian.com, January 15, 2016. http://www.smithsonianmag.com/smithsonian-institution/raoul-wallenbergs-biographer-uncovers-important-clues-his-final-days-180957837.

Gross, Daniel A. "The U.S. Government Turned Away Thousands of Jewish Refugees, Fearing That They Were Nazi Spies." Smithsonian.com, November 18, 2015. http://www.smithsonianmag.com/history/us-government-turned-away-thousands-jewish-refugees-fearing-they-were-nazi-spies-180957324.

History on the NET. "World War Two Timeline." July 10, 2014. http://www.historyonthenet.com/world-war-two-timeline-2.

International Raoul Wallenberg Foundation. Retrieved March 5, 2017. http://www.raoulwallenberg.net.

Paldiel, Mordecai. *Diplomat Heroes of the Holocaust*. Jersey City, NJ: KTAV Publishing House, Inc., 2007.

Rothschild, Amanda J. "The Forgotten Whistle-Blowers Who Saved Jewish Lives." *Boston Globe*, November 1, 2015. https://www.bostonglobe.com/ideas/2015/10/31/the-forgotten-whistle-blowers-who-saved-jewish-lives/6OwS5uDZj1pYHqCL0IG81N/story.html.

Skoglund, Elizabeth R. *A Quiet Courage*. Grand Rapids, MI: Baker Books, 1997.

United States Holocaust Memorial Museum. Retrieved March 10, 2017. https://www.ushmm.org.

Wallenberg, Raoul. *Letters and Dispatches 1924–1944*. First ed. New York, NY: Arcade Publishing, 1987.

INDEX

About the Author

Lisa Idzikowski is a writer, history enthusiast, and biologist from Milwaukee, Wisconsin. While writing about the heroic life of Raoul Wallenberg, she discovered connections to the story through experiences of close relatives who had lived near or visited World War II sites, including Auschwitz. As an educator and author of several nonfiction books for children, Idzikowski enjoys digging into research and capturing the excitement of history for her readers.

Photo Credits

Cover, p. 5 Keystone/Hulton Archive/Getty Images; cover (background) Universal Images Group/Getty Images; p. 7 catwalker/Shutterstock.com; p. 9 Jonathan Nackstrand/AFP/Getty Images; p. 11 Pictorial Press Ltd/Alamy Stock Photo; p. 13 Bridgeman Images; p. 15 AFP/Getty Images; p. 17 Atomic/Alamy Stock Photo; p. 19 Universal History Archive/Universal Images Group/Getty Images; pp. 21, 35 Laski Diffusion/Hulton Archive/Getty Images; pp. 22–23 Leonard Zhukovsky/ Shutterstock.com; p. 25 Keystone-France\Gamma-Keystone/Getty Images; pp. 27, 39 Wojtek Laski/Hulton Archive/Getty Images; p. 28 Apic/Hulton Archive/Getty Images; p. 31 East News/Hulton Archive/Getty Images; p. 33 Imagno/Hulton Archive/Getty Images; p. 37 Telefilm Wallenberg: A Hero's Story avec Richard Chamberlain (Raoul Wallenberg) 1985/Bridgeman Images; p. 41 dov makabaw sundry/Alamy Stock Photo; cover and interior pages designs (stars) f-64 Photo Office/amandaimagesRF/Thinkstock, (radial) ISO100/Shutterstock.com.

Design: Brian Garvey; Layout: Ellina Litmanovich;
Editor and Photo Researcher: Heather Moore Niver